FAMILY ABUSE

Why Do People Hurt Each Other?

Keith Greenberg

Twenty-First Century Books

A Division of Henry Holt and Company
New York

Twenty-First Century Books
A division of Henry Holt and Company, Inc.
115 West 18th Street
New York, New York 10011

Henry Holt® and colophon are trademarks of Henry Holt and Company, Inc.
Publishers since 1866

Published in Canada by Fitzhenry & Whiteside Ltd.
195 Allstate Parkway, Markham, Ontario L3R 4T8

Printed in the United States of America

All first editions are printed on acid-free paper ∞.

Created and produced in association with Blackbirch Graphics, Inc.

Library of Congress Cataloging-in-Publication Data

Greenberg, Keith, 1959-
    Family abuse : why do people hurt each other? / Keith Greenberg. — 1st ed.
       p.   cm. — (Issues of our time)
    Includes index.
    ISBN 0-8050-3183-9 (acid-free paper)
    1. Family violence—United States—Case studies—Juvenile literature. 2. Abusive
parents—United States—Case studies—Juvenile literature. 3. Victims of family
violence—United States—Case studies—Juvenile literature.
[1. Family violence. 2. Child abuse.] I. Title. II. Series.
HQ809.3.U5G74   1994
362.82'92—dc20
                                                                    93-41867
                                                                       CIP
                                                                        AC

Contents

1

The Silent Plague

James Pierson seemed nothing less than a concerned father when he walked into his youngest daughter's bedroom on the morning of February 5, 1986.

Beneath the covers, surrounded by dolls and teddy bears, eight-year-old JoAnn was barely awake. "See you later, peach," Pierson said, kissing the girl on the forehead. JoAnn then responded by giving her father a big hug.

Pierson next entered the bedroom of his older daughter, 16-year-old Cheryl. "Are you awake?" he asked, mindful that this was a school day.

Cheryl grumbled something.

"Now, don't fall back asleep," he reminded her. He then proceeded to leave the home he'd

Cheryl Pierson arrives at court with her lawyer after pleading guilty to first-degree manslaughter. Having suffered years of sexual abuse, Cheryl hired a high school classmate to murder her father.

shared with his two girls and his 21-year-old son, James, Jr., since his wife died from kidney failure.

It was quiet outside in this Long Island, New York suburb, where many had moved to escape the crime of nearby New York City. But Cheryl Pierson hadn't been able to escape her father. She claimed James had been sexually molesting her since she was 11. "I asked him why he was touching me," she would later tell investigators, "and he told me he touched me because he loved me and to never let another person touch me."

Cheryl said she could have "lived with it," had she been the only victim of James's abuse. But, as she grew older and began spending less time at home, she feared that her father would begin focusing his attention on little JoAnn. Cheryl believed she had to do something to protect her sister, so she came up with a desperate plan.

As James Pierson stepped outside the door near the family's kitchen, 16-year-old Sean Pica watched him from behind a tree. Suddenly, Pica revealed himself, took aim, and shot Pierson to death.

Cheryl would later admit that she had paid Pica, her high school classmate, $400 to murder her father. It was the only way she could imagine saving her sister from the humiliation of his sexual abuse. Detectives were sympathetic but they wondered why Cheryl hadn't used another tactic.

"Why didn't you tell anyone?" Detective Jim McCready asked the teenager.

Cheryl's answer mirrored that of victims of family abuse everywhere: "I didn't think anyone would believe me."

A Chronic Problem

Without question, family abuse has been going on forever. It is only in the last few years, however, that many victims have begun to realize that others are willing to listen to them. Around the United States, organizations have been started to end the problems at home—through psychological counseling, arrests, or transferring the abused to safer surroundings. The aim of these

---

Family Violence at a Glance

- Every 47 seconds in the United States a child is abused or neglected.

- About 2.5 million children and teenagers are abused each year in the United States.

- Nearly 42 out of every 1,000 children in America are abused in some way.

- Fathers, stepfathers, or boyfriends are responsible for nearly 70 percent of all child abuse. The remaining 30 percent of child abusers are mothers, stepmothers, girlfriends, and day-care providers.

- Every year, about 4 million women in America are abused in their homes by their husbands or boyfriends. About 25 percent of these cases represent victims who are battered on a weekly basis.

- More women in America are injured by abuse each year than by auto accidents, rapes, and muggings combined.

Source: *The 1993 Information Please Almanac.* Boston: Houghton Mifflin Company, 1993. The American Humane Association.

---

groups is to intervene before a victim is driven to take the same tragic steps as Cheryl Pierson.

Organizations that aid victims have also been able to accumulate statistics about the problem of family abuse—statistics that paint a frightening picture of the American home. Since 1982, child abuse and neglect in the United States has increased by 132 percent. There are some 2.5 million cases of youngsters who suffer from child abuse reported annually. Additionally, an estimated one in three girls and one in seven boys will be molested before the age of 18.

While some children are able to come to terms with these disturbing incidents, others carry the scars forever. Most young runaways and teenage prostitutes today were victims of child abuse and neglect, as were many prison inmates.

In 1992, a survey of 39 states uncovered 1,261 cases of children who died from either abuse or neglect—a 49 percent increase from 1985. Eighty-four percent of the victims were below the age of five; 43 percent were younger than age one.

Between 3 and 4 million American women are beaten up by their husbands or partners every year. It is estimated that a woman is battered in the United States once every 15 seconds.

Additionally, studies indicate that as many as 1.5 million senior citizens are mistreated, either by family or in professional facilities, each year.

Defining
Abuse   Family abuse takes numerous forms: physical, sexual and emotional abuse, and neglect. People of both sexes and all ages are affected. Despite a widespread belief that victims are poor and uneducated, wealthy, educated families are not immune from this epidemic.

Child abuse is any behavior that hurts a youngster's physical or emotional health. Sadly, the child is often harmed by the person he or she trusts most— a parent, guardian, relative, or family friend.

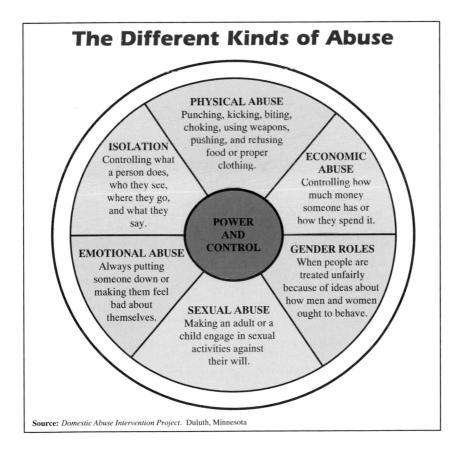

The Different Kinds of Abuse

PHYSICAL ABUSE Punching, kicking, biting, choking, using weapons, pushing, and refusing food or proper clothing.

ISOLATION Controlling what a person does, who they see, where they go, and what they say.

ECONOMIC ABUSE Controlling how much money someone has or how they spend it.

POWER AND CONTROL

EMOTIONAL ABUSE Always putting someone down or making them feel bad about themselves.

GENDER ROLES When people are treated unfairly because of ideas about how men and women ought to behave.

SEXUAL ABUSE Making an adult or a child engage in sexual activities against their will.

Source: *Domestic Abuse Intervention Project.* Duluth, Minnesota

Sexual abuse ranges from nonphysical behavior to extreme violence. Nonphysical sexual abuse includes indecent exposure, obscene phone calls, and "peeping tom" activities—secretly watching a person when he or she wants privacy. Physical sexual abuse occurs when the victim's genitals are touched in some way—through grabbing, fondling, or licking—or when the adult and youngster engage in sexual intercourse. Violent abuse includes rape and other sexually brutal actions. Incidents may occur once or repeatedly, sometimes over many years. The person subjected to sexual abuse almost always experiences embarrassment, fear, confusion, guilt, and anxiety, as well as a general mistrust of adults or strangers.

Emotional abuse is the most difficult type of abuse to pinpoint. The victim may feel insulted, neglected or, in some way, unloved. Day by day, the person is bombarded with negative statements that chip away at self-esteem: unfair criticism, threats, and blame.

Wife and Husband Abuse

Husbands and wives who abuse each other often use a variety of tactics: hitting, biting, scratching, kicking, pushing, choking, and assaults with guns and knives. Victims may have bruises on the face, neck, arms, legs, or torso, and swelling or puffiness of the face or around the eyes. Yet, when these people are asked about their injuries, they will frequently lie. Some lie because they are embarrassed, frightened, or because, for some reason, they want to protect their spouse.

Even when a couple is legally married, a woman can be raped by her own husband. Rape occurs when a woman is forced to have sex against her will. Sometimes, a violent husband will beat and threaten his wife before raping her.

In families where physical and sexual abuse occur, the victim is belittled, and his or her self-worth diminishes. Therefore, the person is also a casualty of emotional abuse. This contributes to a victim's inability to take a stand against the abuse.

Elderly and Disabled Abuse

No form of abuse seems as outrageous as one directed against a helpless person: a small child, senior citizen, or disabled person. All of these individuals depend on family members for their basic needs. Resentment about having to take care of relatives can lead family members to use insulting language and, then, even threats, neglect, and beatings.

In some cases, elderly family members have been confined to one area in the house, denied food, or tricked into signing over money and property. This is especially common when the victim is suffering from Alzheimer's disease, a degenerative disease of the mind. These victims are often disoriented and unable to think clearly.

In recent years, publicity has increased about the sexual abuse of those who have mental disabilities. These people may be adults physically, but mentally they are children. They can thus sometimes be easily persuaded to perform sexual acts. But there have also been cases of adults taking advantage of disabled children or adults who are incapable of reporting the crimes.

Reasons for Abuse

There is never an "excuse" for family abuse, but there are usually many reasons for it. The most common explanation given is that many abusers were themselves raised in abusive environments. As a result, these people grow into adults who believe that methods like physical force are necessary to maintain authority or to exert control.

Some females are emotionally too immature to have children. About 30,000 girls under age 14 become pregnant in the United States each year. These expectant mothers are still emotionally children themselves.

Opposite:
Incidents of child abuse are common among some young parents. Emotional immaturity and economic pressures can often make the frustrations of raising a child too much to bear.

Once the baby is born, when a crisis occurs in the household, they may react immaturely, becoming easily frustrated and violent. This lack of responsible behavior can, in many instances, lead to abuse of infants or small children.

With single parenthood and divorce rates so high, more and more people are raising their children alone, without the help of a spouse. Lacking the emotional support and helping hand of a partner at home, these parents might also feel isolated, cornered, and quick to lash out. In the process, their frustrations can create an abusive environment.

Financial pressures—poor-paying jobs, lack of opportunities for the future, or inadequate housing conditions—can also contribute to stress. A parent's temper may be further aggravated when a child tracks dirt into the house or refuses to sit down for dinner. These small annoyances may cause an already frustrated parent to respond violently.

Drugs and alcohol hurt both the user and the user's family. Substance abuse clouds an individual's ability to reason, and violence sometimes results. In a seven-state survey, researchers discovered that 30 percent of all child abusers were under the influence of drugs or alcohol. As Loretta Kowal of the Massachusetts Society for the Prevention of Cruelty to Children told *Newsweek* magazine, "Crack can turn a loving mother into a monster in ten minutes."

Carrying
the Scars   The scars of family violence are more than just physical. Certainly, the victim can end up with permanent injury, or even die, from violence. But the emotional scars of abuse are also enormous. Depression and feelings of helplessness are frequent. At work, or at school, victims may be so preoccupied with their problems at home that they are fired from their job, or they begin to fail their classes.

Even worse, the cycle of abuse is likely to continue. A husband who abuses his wife may also abuse his children. A woman beaten by her husband may take out her anger on her youngsters or an elderly family member. Children battered by their parents may hit younger brothers and sisters, and may grow up to hurt their own children.

Feeling
Trapped   Why do the victims put up with it? This question is often asked by people who have never experienced the terror of family abuse, and who can't understand that victims see no way out. Some people think that reporting their problem will only anger the offender, causing greater violence. The abuser may be supporting an entire household. That person's spouse fears leaving because the move would put the family in economic jeopardy.

Victims of abuse suffer with a constant sense of helplessness and a loss of self-esteem. These powerful feelings can interfere with the ability to concentrate and to gain satisfaction from life.

Suffering children are too young to try to make a life for themselves, and elderly and disabled victims may depend on the abuser to feed them, bathe them, and take them to the bathroom.

In addition, years of being degraded have worn away the victims' sense of self-esteem. Even if these people *can* make it in the outside world, they've been conditioned to think of themselves as failures, helpless to change their misery.

In the case of a girl being sexually abused by her father, there is commonly great anxiety about separating herself from her family. Too often, mothers take the sides of the husbands or boyfriends who are molesting their daughters, and accuse the girls of "making up stories." A young female who steps forward to expose the horrors of her household faces the risk of losing the affections and financial support of *both* a mother and father.

For too long, family abuse has been considered a private matter. Victims were expected to keep quiet, and outsiders weren't supposed to interfere. Today, the veil of silence is being lifted. Family abuse is a crime. Organizations have been formed to protect and support victims. Just as citizens are responsible for reporting car thefts and home burglaries, they must alert authorities to any suspected incidents of family abuse. In some cases, it's the only hope the victims have of being saved.

2

······

Domestic Violence

Because of their impressive jobs, Joel
Steinberg and Hedda Nussbaum did not seem
typical of couples caught up in domestic violence. Joel was a New York attorney. His
longtime live-in girlfriend, Hedda, had been an
editor of children's books. Neighbors chose to
look the other way when Hedda passed by with
her misshapen face, bruises under both eyes,
and a flattened nose. It was only when the
couple's illegally adopted daughter, Lisa, died
that outsiders got involved.

Steinberg beat Hedda and his daughter regularly and, on November 1, 1987, knocked out
six-year-old Lisa. For years, Steinberg had
convinced his companion that he had special

Hedda Nussbaum holds back tears as she testifies against her former
live-in lover, Joel Steinberg. Steinberg was eventually convicted of
beating his 6-year-old daughter, Lisa, to death.

"healing powers," so Hedda did nothing to revive the child. As the woman sat with Lisa on the bathroom floor that night, Steinberg left for dinner with a business associate. "Don't worry, just let her sleep," he told Hedda. "I will get her up when I get back."

Lisa was still unconscious when Steinberg returned. But the lawyer had other priorities. Instead of taking the child to the hospital, Steinberg and Hedda freebased cocaine. It wasn't until the next morning that Hedda summoned help. Three days later, Lisa died.

Both Steinberg's and Nussbaum's backgrounds made the fact that domestic abuse can occur at all levels of society only

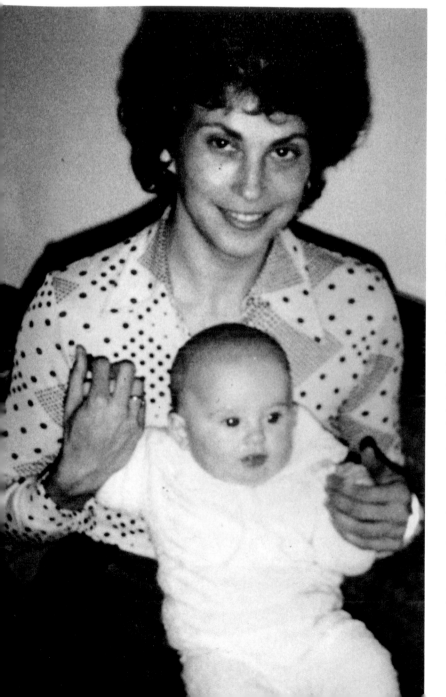

Hedda Nussbaum poses with six-month-old Lisa in 1981.

New York lawyer Joel Steinberg was convicted of murdering his illegally adopted daughter in 1989. The Steinberg case was a sad reminder that abuse can happen in any family, regardless of race or economic standing.

too clear. The same year that Lisa was killed, 899 other children in America died from abuse. "Let's face it," said Dr. Michael Durfee, the coordinator of a child abuse prevention program in Los Angeles, after the murder, "the real tragedy about the Steinberg case is that we've made her (Lisa) into such a story while all the others go ignored."

An Accepted Part of Society

Because of a widely held belief that some form of violence is necessary to keep discipline at home, domestic abuse has been tolerated for too long. In many societies, it is common for men to beat their wives. In the United

An old schoolmaster prepares to administer a beating to an unruly student. A hundred years ago, spankings, beatings, floggings, and whippings were commonly used to discipline children.

States, children have been subjected to spankings and floggings since the time of the first settlers.

Physical punishment was considered the proper way to show disobedient children the errors of their ways. It was not only parents that dispensed beatings, but teachers at school and church as well. In Puritan times, boys were whipped to "drive out the devil" in them. As late as the 1960s, unruly students in many schools were taken to the principal's office to have their knuckles smacked with a ruler. When the children returned home, their fathers were expected to beat them as well, as a further reminder to listen to their teachers.

Why Parents Strike

Why Parents Strike Today, every state has laws prohibiting physical punishment in school, but many parents—both male and female—continue to hit their own children. Thumb-sucking and bed-wetting are among the most common causes for these beatings.

The Debate Over Spanking

A generation ago, in America, just about every child was spanked. Parents never for a moment thought they were committing a form of abuse. Rather, they believed they were teaching youngsters discipline, and the difference between right and wrong.

Despite information that spanking can be dangerous, four out of five parents still believe it is necessary to hit a child, and 50 percent of them spank once a week.

Yet, experts claim that not only can spanking lead to more severe forms of abuse—the hitting will often escalate when the child continues to be defiant—but it simply doesn't work. In an article in *McCall's* magazine, Ron Taffel, the director of a family therapy center in New York, quoted a mother as telling him, "Spanking is the only way I can get through to my child, and lately even *that* doesn't seem to be working."

Taffel believes that children eventually "develop a tolerance" for spanking, sometimes even daring their parents to continue with taunts like, "Go ahead, Mom, hit me. I don't care. It doesn't bother me."

Taffel suggests a less violent, but more direct, form of punishment. He believes, for example, that if a child is misbehaving in a restaurant or at a ball game, the entire family should simply go home.

Additionally, the parents' own troubles can inflame the situation. Alcohol and drug abuse, money problems, homelessness, and a simple lack of knowledge about properly raising children can each contribute to the problem. Since many abusive parents were beaten themselves as youngsters, they believe they are punishing their children correctly.

Detecting
Child Abuse   In many states, teachers are instructed to look for signs of child abuse, and report possible cases to authorities. The following are some of the things they look for:

- Unexplained injuries—in areas not usually bruised during childhood activities: eyes, mouth, back, thighs, buttocks, genitals.
- Unexplained fractures of the nose, face, ribs, legs, and arms.
- Repeated injuries, such as bruises, welts and burns, particularly those shaped like such objects as electric cords, hair brushes, belt buckles, and boards.
- Bruises that seem to have been inflicted for no apparent reason.
- Bruises in a regular pattern, or grouped together.
- Circular cigarette and cigar burns, that are often found on the forearms, hands, buttocks, or soles of the feet.

- Burns in a donut shape, implying that the child was scalded with hot liquid.
- Burns in the shape of an iron, fireplace tool, or heater.
- Friction burns from a rope or cord placed around the arms, neck, legs or torso, indicating that the child was tied up.

The more often injuries appear, the more one should suspect child abuse.

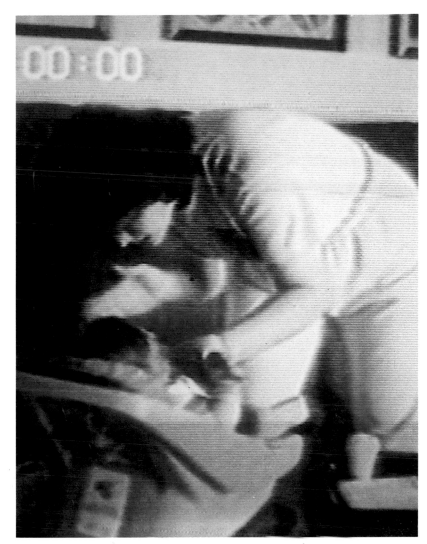

A concealed camera recorded this babysitter as she reached out to slap a small child. Parents must insure the safety of their children when they employ child-care providers.

Abused children may appear hyperactive, overly aggressive, disruptive, or totally withdrawn. It is also possible that they will not communicate with outsiders at all. Occasionally, these youngsters complain of soreness or will move uncomfortably. Many times, they are afraid to go home, and seem to shy away from any type of physical contact.

Shaken Baby Syndrome

For many years, doctors were unaware that some infants that were brought into their offices were suffering from a form of abuse. Shaken baby syndrome—the violent shaking of a small child to stop him or her from crying—can result in convulsions, brain swelling and damage, mental retardation, blindness, and sometimes death. Because studies of this phenomenon are relatively new and inconclusive, little statistical information is available.

Shaking a baby is dangerous because the neck muscles are underdeveloped, and brain tissue is particularly fragile. When a small child is jarred, the brain is repeatedly pulled in different directions, and brain cells tear.

Experts say there are many safe ways to stop a baby from crying, including running a vacuum cleaner, placing the child on top of a running clothes drier while soothing it (most babies like the vibrations), or simply giving the infant a pacifier.

When questioned, parents may deny that anything is wrong. Some will offer peculiar explanations for their child's injuries, or take a long time to seek medical treatment. To hide injuries, parents might dress their youngsters in long-sleeved clothing, even in warm weather.

Husband Abuse

When most people think of domestic violence, they picture a woman as the victim. Most of the time, this scenario is true. However, men can also be abused by their spouses. Because of their embarrassment about being labeled a "wimp," very few husbands report these cases. This secretive situation makes it difficult to study or determine the true seriousness of the problem.

While husband abuse is an important issue, it is not as widespread as wife abuse. Because men are generally stronger than women, and play a more powerful role in many relationships, women are more likely to be battered. When retaliation against men does occur, however, it is frequently with the use of deadly weapons—those that equalize the physical advantages that men have over women.

Who Is the Battered Woman?

Any female can fall into the category of a battered woman. As the Steinberg case painfully showed, education and professional achievement matter little. What's most distressing about the predicament is that too many women assume they somehow "deserve" this treatment. They have been raised to believe that they must

---

Long–Term Effects of Violence and Abuse at a Glance

- A high correlation has been found between people with histories of abuse and those who commit abuse. About 45 percent of all women investigated for child abuse are victims of abuse themselves.

- More than 30 percent of children from violent homes will grow up to be abusers themselves.

- A number of recent studies have established a strong correlation between juvenile delinquency and child abuse. From 26 to 60 percent of all institutionalized juvenile offenders have official histories of child abuse.

- Roughly 30 percent of first and second graders who witnessed violence at home showed clinical signs of depression, nightmares, and other behavior problems such as anxiety, social withdrawal, and physical complaints.

Source: *The 1993 Information Please Almanac.* Boston: Houghton Mifflin Company, 1993.

---

keep their families together at any price. When their husbands are unhappy, the women think they've failed as wives and mothers.

Also, there are many in our society who are quick to blame the victim, saying, "She asked for it," or, "She had it coming to her."

For women who married young and have no job skills, leaving an abusive husband—and the money he can provide—is especially hard. Rather than thinking that she is freeing herself from violence, the battered woman frequently fears exposing herself or her children to financial hardship.

There are also confusing feelings of love that the woman may still have for her husband. While many of these victims want the abuse to end, many of them also want to maintain their relationships. When a woman finally does muster the courage to leave an abusive situation, she exposes herself to taunts from others such as, "If it was so bad, why did you stay with him for so long?"

In the Steinberg case, Hedda Nussbaum had been isolated from her family, and was convinced that her partner had a solution for everything. This is not an unusual scenario. Men who beat their partners may be possessive of them, too. They may cut their partners off from other people. If the woman does consider leaving, she may be threatened with further violence or even death.

The Profile of a Batterer

- Research has shown that a high percentage of victims and assailants were victims of abuse as children. An even higher percentage had parents who were violent toward each other.

- About 70 percent of all spouse abusers who were brought up on criminal charges have some sort of drinking problem. About 65 percent use street drugs, and 35 percent use drugs daily or weekly.

- The most common personality traits of a batterer are those of denial and blaming the victims for abuse. Most batterers also suffer from low self–esteem and thus have a very strong need to control something or someone in their lives.

- Eight out of ten batterers engage in violence against multiple targets, which can include children, girlfriends, spouses, parents, and even pets.

- More than 50 percent of spouse abusers also abuse their children.

Source: *The 1993 Information Please Almanac.* Boston: Houghton Mifflin Company, 1993.

Who Is The Batterer?

The man who beats his wife can be anyone; black, white, Asian, or Native American; a college professor or a drug dealer, a popular person with many friends, or a strange recluse. Often, though, he exhibits at least one of the following traits:

- Possessiveness and jealousy.
- Denial of the violence and its effect on the victim and family.
- Refusal to accept responsibility for the violence, blaming it on alcohol, drugs, stress, or the victim.
- A belief that men should dominate women.

A Town Supports Boys Who Killed Their Abusive Father

People in the small town of Rock Springs, Oklahoma could tell there was something wrong in the Dutton home. Lonnie Dutton, a so-called "town bully," lived with his three sons and daughter in a trailer without electricity and running water. The unemployed roofer would not allow his children to go anyplace but school. Classmates were not permitted to come over for visits.

When social workers saw bruises on the Dutton kids and asked about them, the kids denied anything was wrong. Lonnie Dutton's sister Linda Munn recalled, "They learned, 'If I cry, I get hurt.' They dared not tell."

On July 12, 1993, Herman Dutton—who had recently graduated from eighth grade—and his brother Druie—who had just finished fifth grade—used a deer rifle to kill their father as he lay sleeping on the family sofa. When police arrived, the boys claimed someone else had shot their father. But, soon, they broke down, admitting that they couldn't take his beatings—or his sexual abuse of their ten-year-old sister Alicia—anymore.

People in the town of 1,400 instantly rallied behind the boys. A group of mothers stitched blue ribbons for people to wear in support of the youngsters. When the boys appeared at a court hearing, a caravan of dozens of vehicles drove 18 miles, displaying bumper stickers proclaiming, "Friends of Herman and Druie Dutton — We Support You!"

Everyone in the town wishes they could have done something sooner to save the youngsters. But a deputy sheriff sadly admitted to *The New York Times,* "It all comes down to the child has to be willing to talk. We have gone out and investigated calls, but when we get out there and they won't tell us anything, there's nothing we can do. Many times when you talk to children, they're afraid you'll separate them from their family, people won't believe them, or when they get back they'll get smacked around even harder for telling."

Herman and Druie Dutton with their lawyers, James Perceval and Robert Perrine.

In many cases, the batterer has grown up as part of a family in which parents hit when there is a problem, instead of calmly talking things out to find a solution. As a result, the batterer may have low self-esteem and could have learned that violence was a way to assert instant control over the household. After he lets out his rage, he may feel sorry, apologize, and promise that "it will never happen again." However, this vow is rarely kept. The cycle of abuse is extremely tough to break without professional psychological help. Even with the help of counseling, it may take a long time for a batterer to be able to effectively change the patterns of abusive behavior.

Preventing
Domestic Violence
The best tool against domestic violence is recognizing it for what it is: a criminal act. People must not resign themselves to believing that this is a "natural" part of family life. Batterers should be held responsible for their actions. Victims should attend counseling sessions to restore their self-esteem. Sadly, if feelings of low self-esteem are not successfully erased, it is more than likely that the next time a victim has a relationship, it will be with a person who is equally abusive. The best weapons for fighting abuse are knowledge and self-confidence.

3

Emotional Abuse and Neglect

"You disgust me!"

"You're pathetic! You can't do anything right!"

"You can't be my kid!"

"Hey stupid! Don't you know how to listen?"

"I'm sick of looking at your face!"

"I wish you were never born!"

From time to time, every parent loses his or her temper, but experts say that these comments should never be uttered. Words said in anger cut deeply into children, who look to their parents for guidance as well as support. The youngster on the receiving end of these insults feels unloved and alone.

Children of single parents are especially vulnerable to verbal abuse, since there is no

Severe emotional abuse can cause long-term psychological damage and can devastate a victim's sense of self-worth.

other adult in the house to offer reassurance that things are not as bad as they seem.

Of all the hurtful statements, "I wish you were never born," is probably the worst. Experts say that every person has two basic fears: of failing and of being abandoned. When a parent expresses regret about raising a child, the youngster feels completely unwanted. While the parent may forget making the remark once the situation has calmed, the child is likely to be plagued by the words for a long time.

Verbal abuse is a form of emotional abuse. It chips away at a person's self-esteem over time. Parents use it against children, husbands against wives, and wives against husbands. For many years, few people viewed verbal abuse as a problem. After all, people reasoned, it was better than hitting. But most acts of family violence occur after some form of verbal abuse, so it can be argued that cruel words can lead to cruel actions.

In addition, victims of emotional abuse start to believe what they hear. One Boston woman was called "fat" so often by her husband that she bought clothing four sizes too large for herself. She had become convinced that she was extremely heavy.

Children who suffer emotional abuse grow into adults who look at themselves as the abuser described them. For instance, if a father constantly tells his daughter she is stupid, the girl may not think she has the skills required to go to college. At work, the young girl won't volunteer her opinions, believing that she's probably wrong. A boy who has been told he's ugly may withdraw from people, assuming that they will automatically reject him.

Types of Emotional Abuse

Emotional abuse takes many forms. Aside from verbal abuse, a parent can punish a child by cruelly denying much-needed affection, encouragement, and attention.

One emotionally abusive punishment is "close confinement," limiting a child's movement to a very small area. Tying his or her hands and feet, binding the child to a chair or bedpost, or enclosing the youngster in a closet or other small space are all examples of close confinement.

Every child is entitled to life's necessities. Even prison inmates are given three balanced meals a day and allowed to sleep each night. To deny a youngster the essentials of food or rest is a serious form of emotional abuse.

Failure to act as a qualified parent is another form of abuse. A parent is expected to set limits on the child's behavior in order to guarantee that he or she will grow up correctly. Every child should get the best education possible, and a parent permitting a youngster to stay home because he or she "doesn't feel like going to school" is also committing a type of emotional abuse. This too-relaxed attitude may result in the student being held back a grade, or dropping out entirely.

Even more harmful is the parent who permits—and sometimes encourages—a child to engage in drug or alcohol abuse, which then vastly increases the likelihood that the youngster will grow into an addicted adult.

Even in the best of families, childhood is a difficult time, filled with anxieties about being liked and accepted. From time to time, these pressures drive a youngster into a severe depression, or even bring about a suicide attempt. When this occurs, the parent is obligated to find psychological counseling for the child. If this step is not taken, the parent may be further injuring the youngster's already fragile emotional health.

Signs of
Emotional Abuse
Because emotional abuse is the most difficult type of family abuse to define, it is not always easy to spot a victim. However, there are certain indicators. In the case of verbal abuse, the victim may use the same harsh language on others to belittle them. At home, he or she may sleepwalk or have trouble falling asleep. In school, children are likely to exhibit "extreme behavior,"

lying, stealing, and fighting constantly. They may immediately attach themselves emotionally to new acquaintances, or refuse to play with anybody.

Throwaways   "Throwaways" are young people—usually teenagers—ordered out of their homes or abandoned. When a child runs away, and the parents don't bother searching for him or her, the youngster also becomes a throwaway.

More than 100,000 children become throwaways each year in America alone. These children often fall prey to drug use and resort to crime in order to survive.

Generally, throwaways are kicked out by parents who say, for one reason or another, they "can't take it anymore." Deserted by their families, throwaways have a particularly rough time on the streets. Feeling unloved, they are prime candidates for drug abuse and suicide.

An extensive study, completed in 1988, uncovered 127,100 throwaways in America. This does not include the many children sent to boarding schools and

relatives' homes for the sole reason that their parents simply refuse to raise them. Although these youngsters don't have to live on the streets, they still suffer from being emotionally deprived.

Child Neglect

Parents who neglect their children fail to give them basic shelter, food, clothing, and medical care. Parents too poor to afford these essentials are not considered abusers. But adults who simply don't care about their children's health, schooling, and happiness, are those who are truly guilty of abuse.

Lack of sleep causes many neglected children to fall asleep in class. Hunger can make a pupil steal food from classmates or beg them for sandwiches or sweets. Simple illnesses can turn into serious problems when a sick child is not brought to a doctor. With parents' interests elsewhere, the neglected youngster may regularly come to school late or not show up at all. These students are at a high risk of dropping out or turning to drugs as a means of escape.

Often, a neglected child is alone for long periods of time, and might face dangerous situations without the aid of an adult. For example, a five-year-old girl forced to cross busy streets alone, or an eight-year-old boy who is always expected to cook a full dinner for himself, may be victims of neglect.

Runaways

Children run away from home for various reasons, many having to do with family abuse. Youngsters who've been beaten or raped by family members, or humiliated with constant verbal abuse, sometimes see no other alternative than living on the streets.

Between 1 million and 1.3 million American teens run away each year. The exact figure is hard to pinpoint because many parents do not report their children missing. The majority of runaways never travel more than five miles from home, and 85 percent eventually reunite with their families.

Jennifer is a typical case. Her mother was guilty of both violence and neglect. As a child, Jennifer's head was put through windows, and she was beaten with a baseball bat. Her mother started giving her drugs and alcohol as early as age five.

At age 14, Jennifer left home. By that point, she had substance abuse problems, and lived at drug dealers' houses. For money, she stole cars and burglarized homes. "All I lived for was getting high," she told *Teen* magazine in an interview.

Once, she was shot in the leg. On two other occasions, she was raped. When her friend overdosed and died in her arms, Jennifer decided to stop taking drugs. She moved into a special shelter for runaways, where treatment was offered.

Because of the physical and emotional abuse at home, Jennifer wouldn't consider moving back with her mother. Instead, she set her sights on joining the army and getting a college scholarship.

"Running away doesn't solve anything," Jennifer said. "In fact, it creates new problems. As a runaway, you run the risk of being raped, being forced into prostitution or violence, and using drugs...I feel lucky just to be alive."

Many young runaways must turn to prostitution as their only means of support on the streets.

There are many ways to spot neglected children. Some of them have lice and look malnourished. Others come to school sick, dirty, and hungry. Homework assignments are rarely completed because there is no one at home to supervise the youngsters' activities.

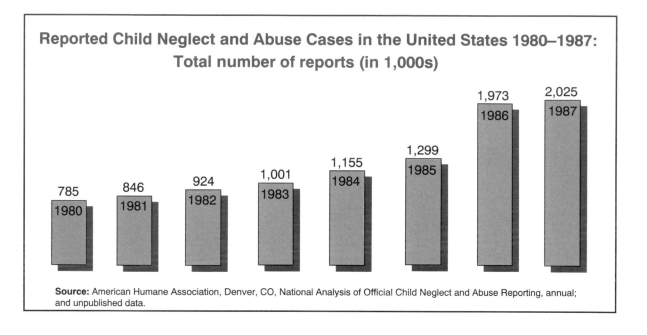

Reported Child Neglect and Abuse Cases in the United States 1980–1987: Total number of reports (in 1,000s)

Year	Reports
1980	785
1981	846
1982	924
1983	1,001
1984	1,155
1985	1,299
1986	1,973
1987	2,025

Source: American Humane Association, Denver, CO, National Analysis of Official Child Neglect and Abuse Reporting, annual; and unpublished data.

Elderly Neglect

Children aren't the only ones that can be neglected. Other people with special needs—the disabled and the elderly, for instance—sometimes do not get the care they deserve.

One of the most shocking cases of elderly neglect occurred in Houston, Texas, in June 1991. There,

70-year-old Margaret Embrey arrived at the emergency room of Ben Taub General Hospital suffering from dehydration and malnutrition. The woman weighed just 95 pounds, 40 pounds less than six months

Physical and emotional abuse of the elderly is a growing problem. As science and technology lengthen average lifespans, there will be more and more elderly members of society.

earlier. She was covered with bedsores, and maggots crawled in her wounds.

Because of a law the state had recently passed regarding neglect of the elderly, Embrey's granddaughter Michelle Ruiz and her husband Adalberto were arrested and charged with criminal abuse. Authorities accused them of not giving Embrey sufficient food, fluid, and medical treatment. Embrey was also not bathed and was not regularly turned in her bed.

The Texas law—among the toughest in the United States—requires that anyone who accepts the legal responsibility for a child, an invalid, or a person over 64 years old must provide the proper care. Linda Mazzagatti, the woman that Texas appointed as Embrey's guardian after her granddaughter's arrest observed, "If not out of love and respect, people will take care of the elderly because of the law."

4

Sexual Abuse

Something seemed to be wrong with Tracy. After school every day, the 16-year-old would dart into her room and close the door, only coming out for a quick meal. She did not have friends, and often said she was not pretty. Her mother, Janet, worried about the girl for months before pleading, "You have to tell me what's the matter, Tracy, or I'll have to send you to a psychiatrist. I just can't take it anymore."

Tracy's response shocked her mother. The girl burst into tears and confessed that, six years earlier, she had been sexually abused by her stepfather. Janet's former husband Michael would fondle Tracy in the bedroom after her bath or as they watched television. Tracy did

Incest is the most common form of sexual abuse. Some studies estimate that 1 out of every 20 people in America has been a victim of incest.

not resist her stepfather because her biological father had abandoned the family, and now she wanted to please this man she called "daddy." Since that time, the girl had carried her secret, filled with guilt and shame.

Janet not only felt sympathy for her daughter, but surprise that no sign of incest had ever been evident. (A sexual relationship between two members of the same family is called incest. These kinds of situations are usually against the wishes of one of the two people involved.) But when Janet finally began to search her memory, she came up with several disturbing images.

Many times, when the family watched television at night, Janet would sit alone on a chair, while her daughter and husband cuddled together on the couch. "When I look back, my father never lay on the couch with me, watching TV," Janet recalled in a March 1989 interview in Canada's *Chatelaine* magazine. "Why did I accept it? Maybe I just wanted Tracy to have a father so much, for us to be a family, that I thought that this was the way things were supposed to be. Maybe Tracy picked up that feeling from me."

Astonishingly, most cases of child sex abuse are similar to Tracy's. About 85 percent of the abuse is committed by a male the child knows well, and half of the molesters are family members. Furthermore,

Sexual Abuse in America

- One out of every 20 people has been a victim of incest.

- Of all the reported cases of sexual abuse and incest, women are most often the victims. One out of 10 women is a victim of incest by the time she is 18.

- By 1986, sexual abuse had become more common than either minor physical abuse or emotional abuse.

- The average victim of sexual abuse is 8 to 15 years old. The average age of the abuser is 21 to 36 years old.

- In 1990, there were 128,000 reported cases of sexual abuse.

Source: The American Humane Association.

the majority of incidents take place at home—not in day-care centers, as many people imagine.

Janet acted the way a mother should when she made the horrible discovery. She told Tracy that she believed her and cared deeply about her suffering. Then, the two entered a special eight-week therapy program for child sex abuse victims and their mothers.

Unfortunately, most other mothers do not show the same understanding. Some accuse their daughters of making up stories, or somehow "asking for" the abuse. Husbands frequently persuade their wives to turn against their children. When social workers question the women about the need to move abused children to safer homes, many mothers lie, saying that everything is fine. As a result, victims remain in the same house with the abuser, only to suffer again and again. When police attempt to arrest the abusive men, many wives choose to flee with their husbands, while leaving their children behind.

In the 1980s, reports of sex abuse in the United States tripled. Some say that this is because more people are willing to speak out. Even if this is the case, there are thousands of victims despairing in silence.

Pedophilia   Translated from Greek, the term pedophilia means "love of children." A "pedophile" is a person who takes pleasure in engaging in sexual activities with youngsters, particularly those who have not yet reached puberty. The typical abuser's appetite for sex is constant. It is estimated that the average pedophile molests a total of 380 children in a lifetime.

Most pedophiles are male. Generally, the abuser is not a stranger in town or a "weirdo." In many cases, he is a scout leader, clergyman, uncle, coach, or other well-respected member of the community. These people may have problems relating to adults because of some childhood incident that prevented their emotional development. Often, this episode was sexual abuse—40 percent of the men who molest boys and 24 percent of the men who molest girls were themselves molested as children.

There are three standard types of pedophiles:

Aggressive: A violent attacker who might mutilate or physically beat his victims after sex. This is the rarest kind of molester.

Fixated: An abuser who seems to live for his next sexual experience. Although he may sometimes feel guilty, he justifies his actions by claiming that he's offering badly needed companionship to lonely children.

Regressed: The most common type of pedophile. This is frequently a married man with children of his own. But when a stressful situation arises— such as the loss of a job—he relieves his anxiety by seeking sex with a child.

What pedophiles in all three categories have in common is that they crave "a sense of power that is lacking in their lives," said Geral Blanchard, a Wyoming therapist and expert on sex offenders, in an

Pedophiles are most often men who have gained the trust and respect of children. Those bonds are then violated by pedophiles when they engage in sexual activities with those youngsters.

April 1992 *Redbook* article. By taking advantage of a child, they momentarily feel that power. However, the sensation doesn't last very long, and soon they pursue other children.

Some pedophiles target girls, others seek boys. But, to many abusers, the gender of the victim doesn't matter. They are simply attracted to children, regardless of sex.

Sadly, children abused and neglected at home are most vulnerable. Ross Nelson, a child molester serving a 20-year sentence in Texas, told *Redbook*

Children Who Abuse

Danny's young life had been filled with pain. He'd been sexually abused by his mother, grandmother, and uncles. And, by age six, he was copying that behavior. After being sent to a special home for molesting his younger half-sister and half-brother, Danny returned to his neighborhood, where he dragged a three-year-old into a garage and sexually abused him.

As astonishing as the story sounds, Danny's conduct is not uncommon. While much emphasis has been placed on adults who molest children, youngsters who become abusers themselves have received little attention.

Many, like Danny, are victims of abuse who are trying to feel less helpless by forcing someone else to suffer the same experience. Although every case is unique, some children come from families with such problems as alcohol, drugs, divorce, or neglect. Although the majority of young abusers are boys, a high percentage are girls.

Adults are just beginning to realize the seriousness of this issue. "It's frightening for most people to believe these kids are forming a pattern of abusing other kids as early as three, four, and five," Sandra Ballester, who runs a program for molesters under age twelve, told *Newsweek* magazine.

There are only about 25 programs around the United States dealing with the problem, including Ballester's group, SPARK—for Support Program for Abuse Reactive Kids. Run by the Children's Institute International in Los Angeles, SPARK treats young abusers in a number of ways, including "monster therapy." The children are told that they are not bad, but their abusive behavior is a monster that must be destroyed.

magazine in the same April article that he would seduce a boy by offering him "very little beyond what he should have found at home: someone who'd listen and who'd cheer him on in school and sports. Occasionally, I took boys to the movies or on camping trips, or played cards with them for hours."

In August 1987, Gene Abel, a doctor specializing in sex research, gave *Redbook* an explanation of why boys are generally preferred by molesters: "Boys are taught to be tough, and not tell anyone when they're hurt. Because they know that they are expected to handle tough situations without crying or acting like a 'sissy,' it is often, ironically, the toughest boys who keep the secret the longest."

Some pedophiles are involved with child pornography and take nude photographs of their victims before approaching them sexually. In one case, a teacher asked a student to help him out after class. The student accused the teacher of giving him alcohol and marijuana and asking him to pose nude on videotape. The student also reported that he agreed to have sex with his teacher because he did not want to make his teacher unhappy.

When the police arrested the teacher, they found a total of 650 videotapes, photographs, and picture books at his home. These sexual images of youngsters—examples of child pornography—are often discovered in pedophiles' homes. There are secret

Victims of sexual abuse can be withdrawn and unable to tolerate physical contact with others.

organizations of child pornography collectors around the world, who communicate and exchange material through computer networks and the postal system.

No Cure for Pedophilia

Although pedophiles may stop molesting youngsters after a short rehabilitation, most of them return to abusing children after only three or four years without therapy. Geral Blanchard, the Wyoming therapist, blames this trend on the fact that pedophilia has historically been treated as a criminal problem. He believes that it is an addiction. "Controlling any addiction is a lifelong process," he said. "There's no such thing as a cure. With the right treatment, we have a better chance of managing the behavior over long periods of time." He recommends counseling, group therapy, drugs that restrict the abuser's sex drive, and programs similar to those used for drug and alcohol addiction.

Signs of
Sexual Abuse

In children, signs of sexual abuse often include torn, stained, or bloody underclothing; pain, itching, or bruising in the genital region; difficulty walking or sitting; urinary tract infections; and venereal disease and pregnancy.

The sexually abused child can act overly sexual, or withdrawn and depressed. The youngster may gain or lose a good amount of weight. In homes where a father is molesting a child, victims can also be overprotective of younger siblings, fearful that they too will be hurt. Sudden difficulties might arise in school. Hysterical or highly emotional behavior may seem to come from nowhere. The child might attempt suicide—either to "cry out for help" or simply to put an end to his or her agony.

Offering support and compassion to victims of abuse is one of the most important steps in helping them to recover.

Repressed Memories

Child sex abuse is so disturbing that some children grow into adults denying that the cruelties ever occurred. Many suffer from feelings of shame, but can't understand why. Others sink into depression, eat too much, gamble heavily, or become alcoholics. It is only after beginning therapy that they realize many of their problems are caused by the "repressed memories" of being molested.

In recent years, some of these survivors have attempted to find justice in courtrooms by using their repressed memories as evidence against abusers.

Sharon grew up in Colorado Springs, Colorado, the daughter of an investigator for the district attorney's office who specialized in—ironically—child abuse. Outsiders never would have figured out the reality of the horror in the home. Sharon said her father would regularly beat her brothers and sisters, lining up the rest of the family to watch. "Someone always had a bloody nose, a split lip or bruises," she told *Redbook* magazine in an interview in July 1991. "What could I do? I tried to block it out."

Sharon tried to overlook other memories as well, but always sensed that something just wasn't right in her life. When she wrote her mother that she was seeing a therapist, her mother fired back an angry letter: "You are in areas which I am sure you do not understand...Don't you know that you were not the first one he abused?"

The statement stunned Sharon, but, as she stayed in therapy, she says, old memories came back. One of the victim's most unsettling recollections was being raped by her father at about age four, hearing him say, "You'll never feel like this again until you're married."

Eventually, her sister told Sharon that she too had been sexually abused by their father. As an adult, her sister had been hospitalized for depression and panic attacks. Now, she was planning to sue the father for damages. Sharon decided to join her. A judge allowed the case to proceed, and the sisters were each awarded 1.2 million dollars.

But others say that courtroom evidence from "repressed memories" is less than reliable. Elizabeth Carlson of Minnesota told CBS News during an interview in August 1993, that her therapist convinced her that she'd been sexually assaulted by eight or nine different people. "If you don't remember getting raped, you won't get well," the therapist told her. Now, Carlson claims she was not abused.

The same August, a CBS News report covered the story of Kathryn Hall of Michigan, who sued her father for sexual abuse, claiming that memories of rape emerged in therapy sessions. But it was revealed that Kathryn's therapist had herself been abused by male family members and may have passed on these feelings to her client. A judge dismissed the case for lack of evidence.

Still, adults who come forward with childhood horror stories must be taken seriously. As Ellen Bass, an abuse counselor, stressed during the CBS News report, "The vast majority of recovered memories are recovered from real child sex abuse."

Even after the abuse stops, children may continue practicing the behavior that was taught them by the abuser. One Canadian mother, for example, reported that her young sons engaged in sexual activities with each other after their rapist-father left the house.

Helping the Victim

According to laws and legislation recently passed in North America, physicians, teachers, and social workers are now required to report knowledge of any type of child abuse. The aim is not so much to punish the abuser as it is to protect children from future torment.

If you discover that someone has been sexually abused you should remember the following rules:

- Believe their story, no matter how unbelievable it sounds to you.
- Do not blame, punish, or embarrass the victim.
- Control your emotions. Showing either fear or anger—even if it is directed at the abuser—can alarm a victim.
- Reassure the victim that it is okay to tell you what occurred, and that he or she is correct in reporting the abuse.

Also, victims should visit a physician to check for venereal diseases, pregnancy, or physical injuries. Abuse victims should go to the police to register charges and have the abuser arrested.

5
∎∎∎∎∎∎

Healing

Once a pattern of abuse ends, the victim must then take on the task of repairing his or her life. Sometimes, the person feels the need to confront the abuser. Other times, the victim simply desires the compassion of a close relative or friend.

Donald Bross, an advisor for the Kempe National Center for the Prevention and Treatment of Child Abuse and Neglect in Denver, Colorado, believes that—regardless of the circumstances—most victims feel better when the abuser admits wrongdoing. In cases of physical and sexual abuse, "the victim is made to feel responsible, like they deserved it, like they somehow made the abuser do it," Bross said. To hear the abuser counter that opinion and take responsibility is reassuring.

Unfortunately, many times victims don't gain that satisfaction. That leads the abused to look

Child abuse victims participate in horseback riding activities at the Childhelp ranch in California. A number of facilities, designed to help heal the abused, are available throughout the United States and Canada.

to others for help. Friends, teachers, and therapists can aid the healing by driving home the point that abuse was *not* the victim's fault.

Some people are more vulnerable to being victims of sexual abuse because a part of them needs to be "liked" by the molester. Others have purposely misbehaved because provoking their abusive parents' rage was a sure means of getting attention. But young children may not be able to figure out right and wrong in such complicated matters. Adults, on the other hand, know the difference, and must take full responsibility for treating children badly.

In order to grow up and lead healthy, productive lives, children of abuse must be able to speak about their feelings and experiences. Trained doctors and counselors can provide therapy that will help young victims cope with the future.

Speaking
Up
The most powerful weapon against a child abuser is the word of the victim. However, abused youngsters are hesitant to speak up because of numerous fears.

Can Victims and Abusers Ever Be Friends?

Years after abuse has occurred, an abuser may occasionally ask for forgiveness. A parent who is guilty of abusing a child may want to put the terrible memories of the past behind him or her and carry on a new, friendly relationship with the child.

Is this possible? Donald Bross, advisor for the Kempe National Center is not sure that it is. "No one can ever go back to the way things would have been," he explained. "Trying to completely undo something may not be realistic. Expectations may be too high, and the people may be let down."

Bross also worries that an abuser who wants to be forgiven is not taking responsibility for the victim's pain. "Why should victims have to forgive, unless they're ready to?" he asked. "It's making the victim responsible for a situation that [the victim] didn't create. Too many times, the victims are blamed for the abuse. Asking them to forgive is again putting the responsibility on the victim."

Still, many victims insist that talking about the abuse is the only way to prevent it from happening again. "No amount of money could undo the past," said a woman whose father had regularly molested her and her sister when they were young. But she defended her decision to bring her father to trial years later by saying, "We hope we've given other incest victims courage to speak out."

Coping The abuse always has a damaging and lasting effect on the victim. Coping with this reality is a difficult struggle. Counseling is important for both the parents and the children after an abusive situation has taken place. Discussing and understanding the situation will not take away the anguish completely, but it can at least limit its destructive effects over time.

First Lady Hillary Rodham Clinton (right) and U.S. Attorney General Janet Reno announce the publication of a government-sponsored study on child abuse. Since the Clinton administration began, it has made child abuse prevention one of its top priorities.

Despite therapy, Tracy (the teenager mentioned at the beginning of Chapter 4) suffered a nervous breakdown one year after she told her mother about her molestation. However, she recovered, graduated high school with outstanding grades, and went on to college, where she plans to become a lawyer and help other victims of sexual abuse.

Seeking Justice

Many family abuse victims seek justice years after the events have occurred. For some, this can be a positive experience. Finally, the victims are able to have the chance to tell their side of the story and to hear a judge or jury proclaim the abuser's guilt. However, other victims may be better off simply not reliving the pain of the abuse. It should be remembered that every person is an individual, and each has his or her own thoughts about what they think is necessary to achieve a sense of justice.

Looking

Ahead
Because so many abuse victims go on to continue the cycle with their own loved ones, it is crucial to understand the abuse that has occurred. "Different people experience recovery (from abuse) in different ways," Donald Bross explained during a recent interview. "But they all must be able to turn to someone for the support and caring that was denied them." That way, the bad feelings will not be transferred into relationships that victims have with spouses, friends, or children.

Healing from the pain of abuse involves realizing that bad memories will surface from time to time. Once a person has been wounded, it is hard to forget the pain. If the abuser is a relative, the victim may run into that person, or others who keep in close contact with him or her. Even if the victim never faces the abuser again, he or she may meet a person whose looks, voice, or opinions remind the abuse victim of painful times.

"If you have a disease, it may affect you when you least expect it," Donald Bross said. "The healing process has to do with knowing that something like this will happen. You might be reminded of the abuse when you're not prepared. So you need to develop the confidence to know that everything will turn out all right."

Glossary

battered woman A woman beaten by her husband or boyfriend.

child abuse Any behavior that hurts a child physically or emotionally.

close confinement Limiting a child to a small area, or tying up the youngster.

disabled abuse Abuse of the disabled, including neglect.

domestic abuse Abuse of one family member by another.

elder abuse Abuse of the elderly, including neglect.

emotional abuse Using words or withholding affection to hurt someone.

husband abuse Abuse of a husband by a wife.

neglect Failing to give a child, disabled person, or elderly adult proper shelter, food, clothing, or medical care.

pedophile An adult who has sex with children.

pornography Words or pictures that are meant to cause sexual arousal.

repressed memories Memories that stay buried in a person's mind, either for many years, or forever.

sexual abuse Abusive sexual behavior that ranges from obscene phone calls and indecent exposure to rape.

shaken baby syndrome The violent shaking of a baby in order to stop the child's crying, often causing injury.

throwaways Children who are either forced out of their homes or abandoned by their parents.

verbal abuse Using cruel language and insults to hurt someone.

Where to Find Help

National Child Abuse Hotline
(800) 422-4453

National Center on Child Abuse and Neglect
Department of Health and Human Services
P.O. Box 1182
Washington, DC 20013
(800) 394-3366

National Council on Child Abuse & Family Violence
1155 Connecticut Avenue, NW
Suite 400
Washington, DC 20036
(800) 222-2000

National Committee to Prevent Child Abuse
332 South Michigan Avenue
Suite 1600
Chicago, IL 60604
(312) 663-3520

American Humane Association, Children's Division
63 Iverness Drive East
Englewood, CO 80112
(800) 227-5242

Survivors of Incest Anonymous, Inc.
World Service Office
P.O. Box 21817
Baltimore, MD 21222
(410) 433-2365

For Further Reading

Crisfield, Deborah. *Dysfunctional Families.* New York: Macmillan Children's Book Group, 1992.

Hyde, Margaret O. *Sexual Abuse: Let's Talk about It.* Louisville, KY: Westminster John Knox, 1987.

Mufson, Susan, and Kranz, Rachel. *Straight Talk about Child Abuse.* New York: Facts On File, 1991.

Rench, Janice E. *Family Violence: Coping with Modern Issues.* Minneapolis, MN: Lerner Publications, 1991.

Stewart, Gail. *Child Abuse.* New York: Macmillan Children's Book Group, 1989.

Source Notes

Abel, Gene, G., and Harlow, Nora. "The Child Abuser, How Can You Spot Him?" *Redbook*, August, 1987.

Bennetts, Leslie. "Nightmares On Main Street." *Vanity Fair*, June, 1993.

Bruning, Fred. "An Unnerving Tale of Domestic Violence." *Macleans*, February 27, 1989.

Gelman, David; Gordon, Jeanne; Christian, Nicole; Talbot, Mary; Snow, Katrin. "When Kids Molest Kids." *Newsweek*, March 30, 1992.

Kantrowitz, Barbara. "The School For Scandal." *Newsweek*, August 17, 1992.

———. "And Thousands More." *Newsweek*, December, 12, 1988.

Karlsborg, Elizabeth. "Teens On the Run, What's Really Out There." *Teen*, July, 1992.

Kleiman, Dena. "A Deadly Silence." *Ladies Home Journal*, November, 1988.

Nelson, Ross M., and Fitzgibbons, Ruth Miller. "Why I'm Every Mother's Worst Fear." *Redbook*, April, 1992.

Ohlendorf-Moffett, Pat. "Wives of Men Who Commit Incest." *Chatelaine*, March, 1989.

Rosado, Lourdes. "Who's Caring for Grandma?" *Newsweek*, July 29, 1991.

Simone, Sharon; Hammond, Susan; Mosedale, Laura. "Our Forty-Year Nightmare Is Over." *Redbook*, July, 1991.

Taffel, Ron. "Spanking: Is It Ever All Right?" *McCall's*, September, 1992.

Verhovek, Sam Howe. "Town Rallies Behind Boys Who Killed Father." *The New York Times,* July 25, 1993.

"The Wounds of Words." *Newsweek*, October 12, 1992.

Index

Photo Credits
Cover: Stuart Rabinowitz; pp. 5, 21, 25: AP/Wide World Photos; p. 13: ©Paul Shambroom/Photo Researchers, Inc.; pp. 16, 32, 47, 50, 51: ©Blackbirch Press, Inc.; pp. 18, 20: Charles Wenzelberg/AP/Wide World Photos; p. 22: Northwind Picture Archives; p. 23: ©Spencer Grant/Liaison International; p. 30: J. Pat Carter/Gamma-Liaison; pp. 37, 39: Gamma-Liaison; p. 41: Rogers M. Richards/Gamma-Liaison; p. 42: ©Hans Halberstadt 1985/Photo Researchers, Inc.; pp. 54, 56: ©Matthew Ford/Gamma-Liaison; p. 58: ©Dirck Halstead/Gamma-Liaison.
Charts and graphs by Lisa Willis.